MW01285273

Learning Spanish:

A Fast and Easy Guide for Beginners to Learn Conversational Spanish

Free membership into the Mastermind Self Development Group!

For a limited time, you can join the Mastermind Self Development Group for free! You will receive videos and articles from top authorities in self development as well as a special group only offers on new books and training programs. There will also be a monthly member only draw that gives you a chance to win any book from your Kindle wish list!

If you sign up through this link http://www.mastermindselfdevelopment.com/specialreport you will also get a special free report on the Wheel of Life. This report will give you a visual look at your current life and then take you through a series of exercises that will help you plan what your perfect life looks like. The workbook does not end there; we then take you through a process to help you plan how to achieve that perfect life. The process is very powerful and has the potential to change your life forever. Join the group now and start to change your life! http://www.mastermindselfdevelopment.com/specialreport

Table of Contents

♥ Copyright 2017 by Mastermind Self Development All rights reserved.

The follow eBook is reproduced below with the goal of providing information that is as accurate and reliable as possible. Regardless, purchasing this eBook can be seen as consent to the fact that both the publisher and the author of this book are in no way experts on the topics discussed within and that any recommendations or suggestions that are made herein are for entertainment purposes only. Professionals should be consulted as needed prior to undertaking any of the action endorsed herein.

This declaration is deemed fair and valid by both the American Bar Association and the Committee of Publishers Association and is legally binding throughout the United States.

Furthermore, the transmission, duplication or reproduction of any of the following work including specific information will be considered an illegal act irrespective of if it is done electronically or in print. This extends to creating a secondary or tertiary copy of the work or a recorded copy and is only allowed with express written consent from the Publisher. All additional right reserved.

The information in the following pages is broadly considered to be a truthful and accurate account of facts and as such any inattention, use or misuse of the information in question by the reader will render any resulting actions solely under their purview. There are no scenarios in which the publisher or the original author of this work can be in any fashion deemed liable for any hardship or damages that may befall them after undertaking information described herein.

Additionally, the information in the following pages is intended only for informational purposes and should thus be thought of as universal. As befitting its nature, it is presented without assurance regarding its prolonged validity or interim quality. Trademarks that are mentioned are done without written consent and can in no way be considered an endorsement from the trademark holder.

Introduction

Congratulations on downloading *Learning Spanish: The Best Way to Learn Spanish* and thank you for doing so.

The following chapters will discuss how you can start speaking Spanish fast. This book is based around a method that I've developed and curated alongside and based off of some of the most prolific language learners and educators of the modern age.

Why learn Spanish? Well, I'm sure that if you picked up this book, you already had a reason, but it's worth going a bit more into it anyway. You should learn Spanish because, simply put, it's a rich language.

Over the last several centuries, Spanish has been across multiple continents and forged connections between all of them. Spanish has persisted as a linguistic force since the Spanish empire began to cover the world over. The language spoken now isn't quite the same as the language spoken in the 15th century on the first voyage to the new world, but the similarities between that variety of Spanish and the modern day variety of Spanish sets you up for libraries worth of literature from all over the world in the Spanish language.

What's more is the sheer beauty of the fact that Spanish, since it's covered the world over, has taken in a number of influences from other languages. Through its journey starting as a mere dialectical splinter of Vulgar Latin (the version of Latin spoken by the general populace of the Roman Republic and the Roman Empire), Spanish has picked up plenty of influences from all kinds of different languages and cultures, most notably from Arabic during the Arab occupation of Spain from the 700s to around the thirteenth century, but also from the Goths, the Basques, the Native Americans, and the Celts.

So in other words, when you learn Spanish, you're setting yourself up to be involved in learning a whole wealth of cultural and historical information in what is a relatively passive manner. That sheer attachment to history is one of the most beautiful things about learning language in general.

However, there are a great number of reasons otherwise for which you might learn Spanish. The growth of the Latin American population and the dissemination of Latin American culture into the United States provides an excellent opportunity in two ways. Firstly, you will inevitably be a more attractive candidate for various careers from a perspective of qualifications. Your ability to speak Spanish will make you an asset in more ways than you can possibly fathom, and a huge number of companies will be lining up in order to get you to work with them, especially if you're specialized in another manner too. Secondly, you'll have opened the door to talking to a whole new set of people. No longer will you be relegated to speaking simply to people who know and understand English; rather, you'll be able to speak to and with people from the culturally beautiful continents of South America and Central America and the wonderful Latin American people. It will also enable you to go to travel to Spain with ease and talk to numerous people who are native Spanish speakers and, more importantly, natives to the *region*, which will most certainly help you to understand the culture, customs, and realities of the place that you're in.

I've already mentioned how Spanish is a language with an absolutely colossal reach, and with that in mind, I feel as though it's necessary to make a certain stipulation. Just like the English spoken in the United States, the English spoken in Australia, and the English spoken in England are vastly different, likewise is the Spanish of Spain, the Spanish of Mexico, and the Spanish of, say, Argentina. They're different in manner of accent and dialect and some basic things, such as the usage of "vosotros" in Castilian Spanish (*Castellano*), or the Spanish of mainland Spain, where instead "ustedes" is used in Latin American Spanish. There's also the fact that certain dialects use the pronoun *vos*, which is generally never used otherwise and sounds rather booky and antiquated in the same way that using the pronoun *thou* sounds in English.

There are plenty of books on this subject on the market, thanks again for choosing this one! Every effort was made to ensure it is full of as much useful information as possible, please enjoy! I can guarantee that by the end of this book, you're going to feel comfortable speaking and reading Spanish.

Chapter 1: Spanish - how does it work?

In the United States, there's an institution called the *Foreign Service Institute.* What they do is train people, generally federal agents such as diplomats, in order to be prepared to go overseas in order to promote United States interests. They provide a huge number of courses in over seventy foreign languages and are one of the authorities on language learning in the United States.

The Foreign Service Institute has a list of languages cut into categories based upon how difficult they are for native English speakers to pick up and learn. Languages such as Arabic, Chinese, and Japanese rank among the hardest, being placed in category V: languages which are "exceptionally difficult for native English speakers."

Languages such as Danish, French, and indeed Spanish place, fortunately, in the simplest ranking: category I, which contains languages closely related to language.

A given language makes their way into this category in several ways. For example, they might share similar sentence structure and grammar to English. On top of that, they might share a lot of common vocabulary (many of the languages in category I developed alongside each other.)

What does this mean for you as a student learner of Spanish? Primarily, it means that you should have an easy enough time getting acquainted with the language and finding your way around it.

In fact, there are a laundry list of similarities between Spanish and English. Take this lightly, however. I've said it a million times before across multiple books: you shouldn't focus on the similarities. There are a few reasons for this.

The first major reason for not getting caught up on minor similarities is that eventually you're going to run into what the French call *faux amis* - "false friends." These are words which sound like they would mean one thing in English but mean a totally different thing in Spanish. Take, for example, the word "éxito." This is a Spanish word, and when an English speaker looks at it, they assume boldly that it means "exit", because, well, it looks like it means "exit". The Spanish word for "exit", though, is "salida" - the word "éxito" actually means "success"! Very, very different word.

There are a huge number more true cognates - words which mean exactly what it sounds like between Spanish and English - than false cognates. But that doesn't mean that it's not too easy to hear very common false cognates and think that they're a certain English word when they're not. This stems from two problems: first, it stems from the person making the bold assumption that English and Spanish must have something in common simply because a given word sounds similarly. This is nowhere *near* the truth, as it frankly shouldn't ever be. And secondly, it stems from a lack of looking at the word contextually and trying to truly figure out what it means given the other words in the sentence. The idea of "context" is your best friend when doing any sort of immersion based language learning, so learning to use it at its most appropriate and as often as you possibly can is wholly essential.

The second major reason for not getting caught up on minor similarities is that, frankly, every language has a lot more in common than things that set them apart. Perhaps not in the context of vocabulary - and there are also things among various languages which are particularly niche and neat, such as the Japanese and Korean languages' ideas of "topic markers" - but at the end of the day, languages are far more *similar* than they are different. After all, what is language, really? Language is simply a method of using our ability to speak in order to transmit and process information between one another. It's the apex of human cooperation. In that respect, every language is serving the same purpose: transmittance and processing of given tidbits of information. And all information has something in common: the rational devolution of a sentence into smaller pseudo-concepts. For example, different languages may place them differently, but every single language has a mechanism for denoting the bare linguistic essentials, like subjects (the thing around which the sentence is formed), actions (the things which the subject undertakes), objects (the thing which receives or acts as recipient of the action), as well as various modifiers in order to further and better describe things.

So to get stuck on the similarities between Spanish and English is absolutely absurd, because to point out the similarities is to say things such as "Spanish and English both have *objects*", "Spanish and English both have *pronouns*", and "Spanish and English both have some degree of Latin derivation due to their historical basis from mainland Europe." That's practically useless information in the grand context of language learning.

The things which actually matter in the context of language learning are found in the *differences*. The same basic mechanisms will persist, albeit manifested differently.

So what are the differences between English and Spanish? Well, despite the similarity of the two languages, they're numerous.

For one, Spanish has a very different system of pronunciation to English. It's far more regular but also a fair bit more nuanced in the specific sounds. With the espoused regularity of Spanish pronunciation comes a fair amount of adjustment from our English alphabet where a given letter can stand in for any number of different sounds. What this essentially means is that Spanish offers a far more rigid system of pronunciation which makes it easier to speak and learn, but it also means that you'll simultaneously have to undo some of the pronunciation consistencies that you've subconsciously learned while speaking English, which can be a lot easier said than done. Anyhow. we'll go more into the specific pronunciation of words in the second chapter.

Lesson one: Gendered nouns

Another way that Spanish differs is that it treats adverbs and adjectives far differently than English does. This might not sound terribly menacing at first, but it can definitely be difficult to keep up with early on in you're learning. The reason that it's so weird is because Spanish has something called *gendered nouns.* I'm introducing this concept to you early because it's the one which is bound to trip you up first and, as such, it deserves to be the first concept which you really work with.

Spanish applies genders to every single noun. For example, the word for *banana* is masculine (*plátano)*, while the word for *table* is feminine (*mesa*).

So what does this mean? Does this mean that tables are meant for women and bananas are meant for men? That a woman eating a banana implies that she's doing something not "ladylike"? No, not at all.

The concept of gendered nouns is a purely grammatical concept and has nothing to do with any kind of innate masculinity or femininity of a noun. It's actually a concept which dates back to vulgar Latin, where there were three articles (we'll talk about those in a moment) known as *ille, illa,* and *illud.* Well, they were actually demonstrative adjectives, but that's another discussion entirely. These would be used by the common people in order to refer to specific instances of a noun, and which one you use would largely depend upon the ending sound of the word which came before it. This is a concept known as "vowel harmony". In other words, the concept of grammatical gender is wholly and entirely a solely linguistic concept and has more to do with the harmony of certain phrases than any sort of innate characteristics of the object deciding whether it is "male" or "female". There actually used to be another gender, the *neuter* gender, which was just a third grammatical category for nouns. This gender, however, was dropped with time.

Lesson two: Articles

Articles in Spanish act rather differently to those in English. They correspond specifically to the noun in question in terms of gender and plurality.

English doesn't do this so much. To compare this sort of difference, let's first analyze English's article system.

In English, there are two articles: *the* and either *a* or *an* depending on whether the next work begins with a vowel or a consonant sound. *The* is what's called a definite article, and *a/an* are what are called indefinite articles.

A *definite article* is an article which has a direct correspondence to a specifically stated object in space. For example, take the sentence "have you turned *the* television on today?"

Because of the phrasing of this sentence, you can assume that they're referring to one very specific television which would either be denoted by context (perhaps you're all in the living room and the television won't turn on) or by a clause which specifically denotes which object is being referred to. ("Did you turn the television *in the living room* on today?")

An *indefinite article* is an article which lacks the specificity of the direct article. That is to say that the *indefinite article* refers to a non-specific instance of an object in space. If somebody were to ask you "have you turned *a* television on today?", you would think it was bizarre - principally because when would somebody ask that question? - but you would also likely say "yes" or "no" depending on whether or not you have indeed turned on *any* given television at some point in the day.

This distinction also exists in Spanish, but it's a bit more nuanced.

Spanish has four different *definite articles* which respond to the gender and plurality of an object. For these examples, I'm going to reuse the *banana* and *table* words.

The Spanish definite articles are as follows:

El - singular masculine definite

La - singular feminine definite

Los - plural masculine or mixed definite

Las - plural feminine definite

When I say the "masculine or mixed definite", I mean that if you have a group of people that are of either gender, or objects which are of either gender, then you should use "los". If every given object to which you're directly referring is feminine, then and only then should you use "las".

Spanish also has four different *indefinite articles*. The Spanish articles can broadly translate to either "a", "an", or "some" dependent upon the context.

The Spanish indefinite articles are as follows:

Un - singular masculine indefinite

Una - singular feminine indefinite

Unos- plural masculine or mixed indefinite

Unas - plural feminine indefinite

So how would I relate these to the two nouns I already know at this point? Simple. Let's run through a few basic exercises. Quick reminder that the term for *banana* is *el plátano* and the term for *table* is *la mesa*. Plurality in Spanish works by simply appending an *s*, just like it works in English.

1. Translate "the tables".
2. Translate "some bananas".
3. Translate "a table".
4. Translate "the bananas."

Your answers should have come out as follows:

1. *Las mesas*
2. *Unos plátanos*
3. *Una mesa*
4. *Los plátanos*

The reason that they come out like that is pretty plain. There's not a whole lot going on here, the main things to take away from this lesson is that nouns have specific genders in Spanish, as they do in other Romance languages and a quarter of languages in the world, actually.

There's one more problem we encounter here: the *uncountable nouns* issue. For example, you can eat three peaches, but you can't drink three waters. In the case of an uncountable noun - usually a liquid, but could be any variety of things - you're to not use an article at all.

Lesson three: Subject pronouns

So at the moment, what we're trying to do is form very basic Spanish sentences with a really cursory amount of knowledge that will create a baseline level of Spanish for you to work with going forward.

Sentences in any given language have three basic components, at the minimum: a *subject*, an *object*, and a *verb*. We've covered the basics of introducing objects to your Spanish by covering the bare essentials of nouns and noun gendering. However, in order to do a lot more with this lesson, we really have to critically analyze the whole concept of *subject pronouns* before we can really make our way onto verbs. Spanish verbs are far, *far* more complex than English ones (despite having relatively simpler conjugation rules than a large number of other concurrent Romance languages).

Subject pronouns form the very basis of the most basic sentences. If you don't know what a pronoun is, it is essentially the word which replaces the subject in a sentence.

We make extensive use of this in English, because we really like to talk in the first person. What I mean by this is that if somebody's name were John, and you were having a discussion with him, it would sound terribly awkward if he said "John is going to the store later. John is excited, because John is going to get the stuff to make curry." That simply doesn't work for the way that we structure sentences. We far prefer to *change* those words to the first-person subject pronoun in order to make it sound more accurate and give more context as to who is speaking. This makes fundamentally more sense from a linguistic perspective, too. When we say "I", there's no question about who is speaking - you're referring to yourself. So the distinction between the "I" and actually saying your name is totally unnecessary.

Spanish has these distinctions are well. Spanish actually has a few more of these distinctions than we do - I'll get to that in a second.

The Spanish pronouns are as follows:

Yo - I

Tú - You (singular, informal)

Usted - You (singular, formal)

Él - He/It (masculine)

Ella - She/It (feminine)

Nosotros - We

Ustedes - You (plural) (Latin America)

Vosotros- You (plural) (Spain)

Ellos - Male/masculine or mixed gender group

Ellas - Female/feminine group

Remember that we're working with explicitly Latin American Spanish in this book, and as such, we aren't going to really mess around with conjugating the *vosotros* pronoun. There are three key differences from English in this set-up of subject pronouns.

The first major difference is the separation of the *tú* and *usted* informal and formal pronouns. In English, no such distinction exists. In Middle English it did, as the distinction between *thou* and *you*; however, this has faded away with time as *you* has taken precedence. In case you're unfamiliar with informal and formal pronouns: you use the informal when you're speaking to somebody that you know well, such as a family member or friend, or somebody younger than you. You use the formal when you're speaking to somebody in a position of authority over you, or when you're meeting somebody for the first time.

The next major difference is that Spanish has an official verb for the second-person plural. This is another thing that we don't have in English. This entire idea is actually rather foreign to English. This place is filled by colloquial phrases. In the Southern United States, "y'all" fills the niche; in the Northeast, "youse"; in the Midwest, "you guys". There is not, however, a relatively standardized form, nor is there a singular word. (Even "y'all" is a contraction of the phrase "you all".)

The third major difference is that the Spanish don't have a specific word for "it". The reason for this is obvious if you think about it: they don't have a neuter pronoun or neuter gender *at all*. That concept is missing from Spanish completely in modernity. As such, since every item has either a feminine or masculine grammatical gender, it makes perfect sense to simply use the feminine and masculine pronouns in order to refer to it in a way.

The reason that we're spending a while on this topic is so that you're prepared for the next topic, which will be a lot heavier: *verb conjugation*. But for the concept of verb conjugation, you have to have a subject in the first place to conjugate for.

Without further ado, let's move to the next lesson, which no doubt is of astronomical importance.

Lesson four: Basic verb conjugation (-

er verbs)

So what is verb conjugation? In English, we have a very simplified form. Verb conjugation is simply the changing of the ending of a given verb, or action word, depending upon the person who's performing it. A lot of the verb conjugation in English has fallen away with time. In its place is only a very simple remnant.

Let's take the verb "*to run*" (this form being called the "infinitive") and conjugate it in the present tense.

I run

You run

He/she/it run**s**

We run

They run

The only form of verb conjugation which occurs in the present tense is the adding of the -*s* to the third person singular form.

This is a very different story from Spanish. Spanish is an absolutely beautiful and expressive language. Along with this comes a huge amount of caveats concerning writing and speaking, though.

The heavy conjugation system, however, does have some bright sides. The fact that verbs end differently depending upon who is speaking means that generally, the subject pronoun can (and will) be dropped altogether. This means that sentences are, of course, far more expressive and clear than they often would be otherwise, while also being more economical.

So how do you conjugate a basic present tense verb in Spanish?

Let's look at this using the verb *comer*, meaning *to eat*.

Comer - *to speak*

Conjugation	Meaning	Pronunciation
Yo com*o*.	I eat.	yoh coh-moh
Tú com*es*.	You eat.	too coh-mehs
Él/ella/usted com*e*.	He/she/you eat.	el/ey-yah/oos-ted coh-meh
Nosotros com*emos*.	We eat.	noh-soh-tros coh-meh-mos
Ellos/Ellas/Ustedes com*en*.	They/they/you all eat.	ey-yohs/ey-yahs/oos-ted-ehs coh-mehn

This gives you a very simple summary of how to conjugate a regular -*er* verb in Spanish. There are two other verb forms, which we'll get to momentarily, as well as a slew of irregular verbs, with what are in fact the most common verbs in the language being irregular. We'll also get to those momentarily.

You'll notice in the conjugation table that depending upon who is speaking, the end of the word would change. This is the bare essence of verb conjugation: changing the word in accordance with who is speaking.

There are a whole host of regular -er verbs that you'll find useful. I'm going to give you the conjugation tables for two more, before giving you a bunch of them to practice with.

Vender - *to sell*

Conjugation	Meaning	Pronunciation
Yo vend*o*.	I sell.	yoh vehn-doh
Tú vend*es*.	You sell.	too vehn-dehs
Él/ella/usted vend*e*.	He/she/you sell.	el/ey-yah/oos-ted vehn-deh
Nosotros vend*emos*.	We sell.	noh-soh-tros vehn-deh-mos
Ellos/Ellas/Ustedes vend*en*.	They/they/you all sell.	ey-yohs/ey-yahs/oos-ted-ehs vehn-dehn

Comprender - *to understand*

Conjugation	Meaning	Pronunciation
Yo comprend*o*.	I understand.	yoh cohm-prehn-doh
Tú comprend*es*.	You understand.	too cohm-prehn-dehs
Él/ella/usted comprend*e*.	He/she/you understand.	el/ey-yah/oos-ted cohm-prehn-dehs
Nosotros comprend*emo s*.	We understand.	noh-soh-tros cohm-prehn-mos
Ellos/Ellas/Us tedes comprend*en*.	They/they/yo u all eat.	ey-yohs/ey-yahs/oos-ted-ehs coh-mehn

By now, you should see a very tangible pattern among these. With that in mind, I'm going to give you a few more super common -*er* verbs before we move on to conjugating -*ar* and -*ir* verbs.

Practice verbs:

- aprender: *to learn*
- beber: *to drink*
- poseer: *to possess* or *to own*
- responder: *to respond* or *to answer*
- ofender: *to offend*
- promete: *to promise*

- someter: *to submit*

Lesson five: Regular verb conjugation with -ar and -ir verbs

With the very basics of verb conjugation out of the way, we can now move onto the other verb forms. As I said, Spanish verb forms tend to take three types: *-er, -ar,* or *-ir*. Sadly, a lot of the most common verbs are irregular and don't follow traditional conjugation, but that's just what happens when you have a lot of people speaking a language over a lot of space and saying these words constantly: uniformity falls away to slang as the natural process of linguistic evolution is exacerbated by constant usage. But with that said, the vast wealth of Spanish verbs are indeed regular, they just don't happen to be quite as common. Anyway, we'll get to regular verbs in the next lesson.

The first thing that we're going to cover here is the concept of conjugating *-ar* verbs. We're going to start this process out with the verb *hablar*, meaning "to speak".

Hablar - *to speak*

Conjugation	Meaning	Pronunciation
Yo habl*o*.	I speak.	yoh ah-bloh
Tú habl*as*.	You speak.	too ah-blahs
Él/ella/usted habl*a*.	He/she/you speak.	el/ey-yah/oos-ted ah-blah
Nosotros habl*amos*.	We speak.	noh-soh-tros ah-blah-mos
Ellos/Ellas/Ustedes habl*an*.	They/they/you all speak.	ey-yohs/ey-yahs/oos-ted-ehs ah-blahn

You'll notice that a lot of these conjugations are superbly similar to the same conjugations for -*er* verbs, and you'd be right to notice that. The only major noticeable difference between the two is that these verbs, of course, take an *a* in place of the *e*.

-*ir* verbs act similarly and, in fact, aren't that different either. In fact, their conjugation is exactly the same as -*er* verbs, except for the "Nosotros" form. Observe what I mean as we conjugate the verb *discutir*, meaning "to discuss".

Discutir - *to discuss*

Conjugation	Meaning	Pronunciation
Yo discut*o*.	I discuss.	yoh dees-cooh-toh
Tú discut*es*.	You discuss.	too dees-cooh-tehs
Él/ella/usted discut*e*.	He/she/you discuss.	el/ey-yah/oos-ted dees-cooh-teh
Nosotros discut*imos*.	We discuss.	noh-soh-tros dees-cooh-tee-mos
Ellos/Ellas/Ustedes discut*en*.	They/they/you all discuss.	ey-yohs/ey-yahs/oos-ted-ehs dees-coo-tehn

Indeed, you'll see that there's little to no difference in the conjugation of these *-ir* verbs in the present tense than conjugating *-er* verbs in the present tense aside from the *nosotros* form.

By now, you've conjugated verbs in all forms, so the only thing you can do now is practice. That's how one genuinely and truly picks up skill in verb conjugation. At first, it will be ugly and very much not fun, but after a little practice, you'll be able to do it with absolute ease.

Here are some verbs with which you can practice your conjugating.

-ar verbs:

- caminar: *to walk*
- esperar: *to hope*
- comprar: *to buy*
- ayudar: *to help*
- viajar: *to travel*
- trabajar: *to work*

-ir verbs:

- vivir: *to live*
- debatir: *to debate*
- describir: *to describe*
- unir: *to unite*
- escribir: *to write*
- reunir: *to meet*

Of course there's an endless wealth of Spanish verbs that you can work with, and a little personal research certainly wouldn't be out of the question if you were so inclined. You know how to conjugate these verbs now, and it's on your pto practice it.

Lesson six: Irregular verbs, part one

The hardest part of coming to a new Romance language is frankly not learning conjugation. I've studied quite a few and conjugation comes relatively easy at this point. After all, it's a very finite system with little that ever really changes about it. No, the hardest part is totally and completely getting used to each language's irregular verbs and the numerous idiomatic ways in which they use their irregular verbs.

Given that this is a Spanish book, I won't give you the details all about, say, French or Italian's conjugation system. However, with the fact that it's a Spanish book established, we do need to move on to talking about how to actually conjugate and use these verbs.

The first one that we really need to cover is **ser**, which translates to "to be". It's actually one of two state of being verbs that Spanish has, and between it and the other verb *estar*, the general bases of the verb "to be" as it's used in English are covered.

Of course, the downside of having two verbs for something we represent with one in English is that, naturally, it's more efficient and expressive, but this also comes with the fact that for native English speakers it can be a terribly big adjustment to make linguistically. If you aren't used to representing these sort of ideas using two distinct verbs, then it's going to be a very odd thing for you to start to do so.

So with that said, when does one actually venture out and try to use *ser*? There are a few situations which call for *ser* specifically. The first time in which you'd use *ser* is in situations which specifically refer to things which are essential to you or somebody else's identity. These include things such as any physical description, your personality and your sense of character, the country that you're from, the race that you are, the gender that you are, what you do for a living, and what any given thing in general is made of.

Another time that you'd use *ser* is to

donate any given thing which occurs or takes place at a point in time, such as dates, seasons, events, and time in general.

So how do we conjugate *ser*? Since *ser* is irregular, it'd most likely be easy for you starting out to simply try to remember the following conjugation table, which will come naturally anyhow with practice:

Ser - *to be*

Conjugation	Meaning	Pronunciation
Yo *soy*.	I am.	yoh soy
Tú *eres*.	You are.	too eh-res
Él/ella/usted *es*.	He/she/you are.	el/ey-yah/oos-ted es
Nosotros *somos*.	We are.	noh-soh-tros soh-mos
Ellos/Ellas/Ustedes *son*.	They/they/you are.	ey-yohs/ey-yahs/oos-ted-ehs sohn

So if you wanted to say, for example, "I'm from the United States", that's an intrinsic quality and description of you, so you would use *ser* here. "I'm from the United States" is a nifty sentence because it can actually translate quite directly from English into Spanish.

Yo *soy* de <u>los Estados Unidos</u>.*

I *am* from <u>the United States</u>.

* bear in mind that in conventional spoken Spanish, the "yo" would be dropped since the person who is speaking is implied directly through the verb conjugation.

So with all of that noted, when would we use the other word for *to be*, "estar"? Well, there are a few different cases in which you would use *estar*. It really depends. A good way to remember the usage of *estar* is the following rhyme often taught in high schools: "how you feel and where you are, that is when you use *estar*."

That rhyme, though simple, is not terribly far off base at all. The first usage of *estar* is, indeed, where you are. *Estar*'s principle usage is "emotional and physical states of being". These are temporary things like moods or appearances. This can make quite a massive difference. If you were to say:

Soy enojado.

Wherein *enojado* means "angry", you'd be essential telling the world that you're a very angry person in general. You'd be saying that anger is an essential personality description of you, a permanent fixture of description for you. This is fine if you're, for example, an angsty teenager who is mad at the world or popular multi-million selling rap artist Eminem, but otherwise, you most likely should use *estar*. Using *estar* here makes a world of difference.

When used with emotion or states of being, *estar* can often also stand in for the word "feel" in English: *estar enojado* means "to be feeling angry", which removes the existential burden of being an angry person in general off of your back.

Estar is also the verb that you're supposed to use in order to indicate your location at a given time. Use *estar* in order to say that you're in either this place or that. You can use *estar* in order to denote the location of both people and of things.

So into the belly of the beast: how do we conjugate *estar*? Like so:

Estar - *to be (states of being)*

Conjugation	Meaning	Pronunciation
Yo *estoy*.	I am/feel.	yoh es-toy
Tú *estás*.	You are/feel.	too es-tahs
Él/ella/usted *está*.	He/she/you are/feel.	el/ey-yah/oos-ted es-tah
Nosotros *estamos*.	We are/feel.	noh-soh-tros es-tah-mos
Ellos/Ellas/Ustedes *están*.	They/they/you all are/feel.	ey-yohs/ey-yahs/oos-ted-ehs es-tahn

The distinction between *soy* and *estar* isn't terribly difficult to ascertain once you've got a grasp on it, but it will take two things in order for you to understand nuances like this fully: the first is *practice*. In order to understand how to use these verbs correctly - and indeed, a great number of Spanish words and idioms and phrases in general - you're going to have to practice using them correct. The second is *immersion*. Without proper immersion, you're well doomed. Luckily, modern society makes it very easy to simulate immersion in several different ways, such as watching television shows in other languages or signing up to talk to people who speak another language via services such as italki. Immersion is what allows you to hear the various uses of different phrases and understand how certain ideas and words are used in the context of another language.

Lesson seven: Tenses, part one

There's one more important distinction and usage of *estar* that we haven't really covered yet. Aside from its obvious appearance in Spanish idioms, there's a very important tense that we need to talk about: the present progressive.

Depending on your experiences with other languages, you may or may not be familiar with the common usage of the present progressive. Some languages don't have a present progressive tense in common use, such as French and Danish. English, however, takes great advantage of the present progressive tense.

What the present progressive tense does is indicate an action which is in the process of occurring. For example, if you were studying French, you might run into the sentence "Je chante". This can carry a meaning of either "I sing" in a general sense, or it can carry the meaning of "I am *currently* singing." French has this in a colloquial sense (the phrase "être en train de *verb*" can indicate an ongoing process) but in literature and more formal usage, there is no real equivalent for the present progressive - the simple present tense is used.

In Spanish and English, however, we make this distinction. For example, the phrase "I eat meat" would generally mean that somebody eats meat as a general part of their diet, but by inclusion of the verb "to be" and morphing "eat" into its gerund (the noun form of a verb), we can form the sentence "I *am* eat*ing* meat." which indicates that as we speak, we are eating meat.

Spanish has a very similar system. They too use *estar*, meaning of course "to be", in order to form the present progressive. as well as forming a present participle much like we form gerunds.

The way that the present participle is formed in Spanish is by looking at what kind of verb it is. If it's an -*er* or -*ir* verb, you just drop the ending and replace it with -*iendo*. This means that a verb like *someter*, which we discovered earlier means "to submit", would take on the form *somiendo*. For *-ar* verbs, what you would do is drop the *-ar* ending and replace it with *-ando*. So the verb *trabajar*, again meaning "to work", would become *trabajando*.

So depending upon who is speaking, one would simply conjugate *estar* to the correct form and then stick the present participle after it.

Let's practice! Translate the following:

1) I am working. (trabajar)
2) She is learning. (aprender)
3) You are writing. (escribir)

Your responses should have been as follows:

1) *Estoy trabajando.*
2) *Está aprendiendo.*
3) *Estás escribiendo.*

Are you seeing how this works, a tad? It's a relatively simple tense to form but it can be bizarre.

When you try to form present participles, remember also that not all verbs are created equal. Some, because they have endings which would make appending *-iendo* or *-ando* sound strange, don't have regular endings in the present participle. Be wary of this and, as always, be sure to research constantly as you learn. There's little more important than testing your limits, but being sure that the way you're testing them is correct is definitely up there.

Lesson eight: Working with "haber"

There are quite a few irregular verbs in Spanish. Somewhere close to around 34 percent. And the most common verbs are more likely to be irregular, too, go figure. For example, of the fifteen most common verbs in Spanish, *thirteen out of fifteen* can be described as irregular. It's absolutely absurd.

What this means for you as a language learner is that you are going to have to dedicate yourself to not only knowing normal regular verb conjugations but to knowing how to conjugate the irregular verbs, as well. Some of them have fall into patterns which are easily recognized, such as *hacer* and *decir* or *tener* and *poner*. Others, not so much.

Because of all of this, it can be rather difficult to really know where to start. The answer is that there is not quite a "right" place to start - it's just something that you're going to have to learn as you go on and attempt to use the words or hear the words used.

However, I do think that it's certainly sensible to start with the most *common* irregular verbs first, because you're far more likely to use them on a sentence to sentence basis. So with that said, let's start working a bit more with these irregular verbs and practicing them so that they get mentally tucked away for later use whenever you may need them once more.

The only other major irregular verb that we're going to work with in the context of this book is *haber*. This verb means roughly "to have" (though not in the sense of possessing something - for that purpose, you would use *poseder* instead). *Haber* means "to have" in the sense of the past, which we'll get to in a bit when we discuss more tenses.

Aside from this case (usage as an auxiliary verb), *haber* primarily is used in two other contexts. We'll discuss that after conjugating. Here's how you'd conjugate *haber*.

Conjugation	Meaning	Pronunciation
Yo he.	I have.	yoh eh
Tú has.	You have.	too ahs
Él/ella/usted ha *or* hay.	He/she/you have.	el/ey-yah/oos-ted ah *or* eye
Nosotros hemos.	We have.	noh-soh-tros eh-mos
Ellos/Ellas/Ustedes han *or* hay.	They/they/you all have.	ey-yohs/ey-yahs/oos-ted-ehs ahn *or* eye

Haber - *to have*

So, *haber* when not used to construct the perfect tense usually is used in one of two manners.

Firstly, it may be used in order to say "there is". It's not a direct translation, but if you think about it, it doesn't need to be. "There is" is a nonsensical impersonal phrase. All that it directly implies is the fact that something *is*, in the something *exists*. So *hay* is as much an equivalent phrase in Spanish as *il y a* is in French.

This is simple enough. Let's take that word for banana again, *plátano*. If we wanted to say there is a banana on the table. We'd do this like so:

There's a banana on the table.

Hay uno plátano en la mesa.

It works similarly for doubled objects where we'd otherwise use "There are" as opposed to "There is" in English.

There are three bananas on the table.

Hay tres plátanos en la mesa.

We needed to discuss the usage and implementation of *haber* because that brings us into our next lesson.

Lesson nine: A few more tenses...

I don't think that it would be particularly worthwhile in the scope of a beginner's book intended for people absolutely new to Spanish and perhaps even language learning in general for me to go through every single tense that you might use. My entire goal with this book at large is to get you to understand the underlying grammatical concepts so that you might actually be able to build on them through proper experimentation as well as through constantly trying out new things with the language.

However, there are two more tenses we're going to cover, both of them in the past tense. The reason we're not covering future tense is that for near future verbs, Spanish generally just uses the present tense anyhow, often alongside a time marker. The other Spanish future tense is meant for dates and events which are farther off, and in my opinion as somebody who writes about and works with languages, I don't think that's a particularly paramount subject for new learnings and I don't realistically see time spent on that tense to be worthwhile as a beginner.

What I will talk about however, is the *preterite* and the *perfect tense*.

The preterite is the tense which is used for events which are over and done with; things which happened once already and weren't continuous. This is the one that you need to focus on, and for a very simple reason: you very well may start off a conversation with the fact that you don't speak Spanish particularly well. And if you *were* to do that, you likely wouldn't even need the perfect tense at all. It's not likely or common for introductory Spanish speakers to feel the need to express themselves in the past tense in exclusive or esoteric ways.

If you need to form the preterite with an -*ar* verb, all you have to do is drop the -ar and append the following endings: -é, -aste, -ó, -amos, and -aron.

Here is the -*ar* preterite conjugated for the verb *enviar*.

Enviar - *to send (preterite)*

Conjugation	Meaning	Pronunciation
Yo *envié*.	I sent.	yoh ehn-vee-ey
Tú *enviaste*.	You sent.	too ehn-vee-ahs-tay
Él/ella/usted *envió*.	He/she/you sent.	el/ey-yah/oos-ted ehn-vee-oh
Nosotros *enviamos*.	We sent.	noh-soh-tros enviamos
Ellos/Ellas/Ustedes *enviaron*.	They/they/you all sent.	ey-yohs/ey-yahs/oos-ted-ehs ehn-vee-ah-rohn

Likewise, to form it for an -*er* or -*ir* verb, you just drop the ending and tack on either -*i, -iste, -ió, -imos,* or -*ieron*. Let's try this out really quickly by using the verb *vivir*.

Vivir - *to live (preterite)*

Conjugation	Meaning	Pronunciation
Yo *viví*.	I lived.	yoh vee-vee
Tú *viviste*.	You lived.	too vee-vees-tey.
Él/ella/usted *vivió*.	He/she/you lived.	el/ey-yah/oos-ted vee-vee-oh
Nosotros *vivimos*.	We lived.	noh-soh-tros vee-vee-mohs
Ellos/Ellas/Ustedes *vivieron*.	They/they/you all lived.	ey-yohs/ey-yahs/oos-ted-ehs vee-vee-ehr-ohn

The present perfect tense is very easy. All that you need is the verb *haber* and the verb you'd like to form into the present perfect.

The present perfect carries the same weight as saying something like "I have cooked" or "She has laughed" in English. It's not always a 1 to 1 correlation, but there are a lot of times where the situational usage will certainly match up. And what's more is that forming past participles is absurdly easy in Spanish for regular verbs. All that you do is drop the -*ar*, -*er*, or -*ir* ending and replace it, either with -*ado* for -*ar* verbs or -*ido* for -*ir* or -*er* verbs.

So if we were to take the verb *vivir* again, we

could say "I have lived" in the present perfect tense like so:

(Yo) he vivido.

It's a really simple lesson to take home, but it's an important tense to understand nonetheless.

Lesson ten: one last thing...

In case you didn't know, you obviously can negate things in Spanish. You do so by simply adding *no* before the verb:

Como carne.

No como carne.

The first sentence means "I eat meat", and the second means "I don't eat meat". It's a simple lesson, but infinitely important nonetheless.

Chapter 2: Pronunciation

I'm going to be straightforward as I say this: as a Spanish learner, you have it easy. Spanish has ridiculously easy pronunciation compared to other languages. It makes up for it with difficulty in other areas and a bizarre amount of esotericism compared to other major Romance languages (largely due to Arab influence). However, Spanish pronunciation is simple and predictable. You're hardly going to have a problem with any of it going forward.

The first thing that we need to talk about is the basic vowel sounds. Coming from English, it's really easy to pronounce things like you would in English, especially if it resembles an English word that you know. However, you can't do this. Spanish vowels are absolutely finite in their pronunciation and not saying them correctly is the fast track to sounding like an absolutely inexperienced Spanish speaker.

Here are the vowel sounds for Spanish, alongside how they're pronounced.

a will sound much like the first O in *O*ctober.
e will sound like the *ay* in the word *bay* if the syllable ends in a vowel. If it ends in a consonant, then it will sound like the *e* in *net*.
i will sound like the *ee* in *tree*.
o will sound like the *o* in *rope* if the syllable ends in a vowel. If it ends in a consonant, it will sound like *o* in the word *hot*.
u will sound like the *oo* in *school*, unless

it's in any of the following letter groups: gue, gui, qu. In these cases, it will be silent.

y will sound like the Spanish *i* when it is used as a vowel.

And naturally, Spanish has diphthongs as well. Diphthongs are the resultant sound of two vowels being put together. Generally, in Spanish at least, they're just the end result of the vowels being put together, and you can guess their sound just by putting the two appropriate vowel sounds together rather fast. Here are some common diphthongs regardless, and some familiar sounds you can associate with them:

ai will sound like the *i* in *bride*; **ay** will as well.

au will sound like the *ou* in *sound*.

ei will sound like the *ay* in *gray*; **ey** will as well.

eu will sound like the *ay-you* in *today-you*.

oi will sound like the *oy* in *coy;* **oy** will as well.

u before *any* vowel will sound like a *w*.

i before most vowels will sound like a *y;* **y** will as well.

Now it's time to move onto the consonant sounds. The consonant sounds will in certain places be very familiar, and if so, I'm not going to really bother expounding upon them. However, some are quite different, and so I'll go into detail on those.

B, if at the beginning of a word or when after a consonant, will sound like the English *b*. However, otherwise, it will sound like a mixture between an English *b* and an English *v*. **V** follows the same exact rules.

C, when it's before either a consonant or the vowels *a, u,* or *o,* will have a hard C sound like in "construction". Before the vowels *e* or *i,* however, the **C** will sound like an English *s.*

Ch always sounds the same: like the *ch* in *champion.* The reason I list this as it's own letter is twofold: firstly, English has both a *ch* and an *sh* sound reserved for the *ch* grouping. In Spanish, this isn't the case. However, there's also the fact that throughout history, the *ch* in Spanish has been treated as its own letter, before D but after C. Many older Spanish dictionaries and Spanish-English dictionaries will have the *Ch* words as their own category.

D will always sound like the English *d,* unless it's between vowels or following the letter *l* or the letter *n,* in either case it will be pronounced like the *th* in *that.*

F sounds like the English *f.*

G sounds like an English *h* but with more power, if before an *e* or an *i;* if it's before anything else, it sounds like the *g* in *gather.*

H is silent.

J sounds like an English *h* but with

more power, and is silent whenever it is the last letter in a word.

K sounds like an English *k*.

L sounds like an English *l*.

Ll sounds like an English *y*, though it in some dialects has a slight *sh* sound to it. Pay attention to how the people around you pronounce it and mimic it, but use the *y* sound firstly.

M sounds like an English *m*.

N sounds like an English *n* in every instance except for when it precedes the letter *v*. In this case, it will sound like an English *m*.

Ñ sounds like an *ny* sound, as in *onion* or *bunion*.

P sounds like an English *p*.

Q is *always* followed by *u*, and the pair will *always* sound like an English *k*.

R is performed by way of an alveolar flap in the middle of a word, meaning a very soft touching of the tongue to the roof of the mouth. At the beginning of a given word or when it's following either the letter *l*, the letter *n*, or the letter *s*, it will have a powerful trill. At the end of a word, it has next to no trill, but still a small amount.

Rr indicates a very strong trill.

S will sound like an English *s* unless it's preceding either *b, d, g, l, m,* or *n*, in which case it will sound like an English *z*.

T will sound like an English *t*.

W will nearly always have a *v* sound. There are various linguistic reasons for this phenomenon, but I'm not going to go into them right here.

X sounds like an English *x* is between vowels, but before a given consonant it will sound like an English *s*. This is presuming the word isn't of Native or Aboriginal influence. If so, then it will sound like an *h*. (*Mexico* would sound like *Mey-hee-coh*, and *Texas* would sound like *Tey-hahs*.)

Y sounds like an English *y*.

Z generally just sounds like an English *z*.

As you can see, for the most part, Spanish pronunciation is generally very uniform. When there is a variation, change, or exception, it's likewise generally very easy to understand within the context of the language.

It's also worth noting the role of accent marks in Spanish. In the Spanish language, accent marks indicate *syllable stress* or serve to differentiate one word's spelling from another. This can be of grave importance, as some words without proper accents being written will take on totally different meanings which may at times even be personally embarrassing.

If you see an accent mark while reading Spanish, then it always means that you need to be certain that the syllable with the accent mark is getting quite a bit of stress and is enunciated *loudly* and *clearly*.

You are halfway done!

Congratulations on making it to the halfway point of the journey. Many try and give up long before even getting to this point, so you are to be congratulated on this. You have shown that you are serious about getting better every day. I am also serious about improving my life, and helping others get better along the way. To do this I need your feedback. Click on the link below and take a moment to let me know how this book has helped you. If you feel there is something missing or something you would like to see differently, I would love to know about it. I want to ensure that as you and I improve, this book continues to improve as well. Thank you for taking the time to ensure that we are all getting the most from each other.

Chapter 3: Basic Conversation

I'd be doing you a major disservice if I didn't teach you the very basics of Spanish conversation. The reason I've held off to this point is because a lot of language courses will start off by giving you the basic phrases of a language. That's great for letting you say hello and goodbye to people, but when it comes to building statements with any sort of actual meat to them, it's an uphill battle because you don't actually know anything about the language yet.

For example, before you even picked up this book, you most likely at least knew the word *hola* from having heard it in any number of North American sources involving Spanish speakers. But how much does that matter for having genuine discussion with Spanish speakers? Does that knowledge of *hola* allow you in any capacity to walk up to a Spanish stranger and do anything but say "hello" to them?

The answer, of course, is no. That's an utterly ridiculous notion in most every possible conceivable way. That is thus the very reason that I've held off going over all of this up until now: it simply wasn't necessary and would get in the way of actually *understanding* Spanish in any sort of meaningful manner.

But now that you understand the pronunciation and a lot of basic verbiage, I feel as though we're at a reasonable point where I can give you introductions to conversation without making myself feel like I'm making the language seem like it's anything but what it is: a language, with a thriving set of verb conjugations and unique articles and all of these awesome features that extend far, far beyond "holá".

Anyhow, for the sake of this chapter, we're going to work through a number of phrases one at a time with a brief explanation of everything that we're doing.

The first thing that you do in any given conversation is *initiate* it. Well, this isn't necessarily always true - some people are very pragmatic and get right to the point. But for most people, saying salutations is just a normal part of any given conversation, or perhaps things which aren't even really conversation. Perhaps you're passing by somebody you know in the school or workplace and want to acknowledge them. That's another situation in which you'd find knowing salutations to be a great advantage.

Spanish has a great many salutations and the one that you use depends upon a number of variables, of course.

There's, of course, the general use *hola* (oh-la). This just means "hello" in English. The etymology of the word "hola" is deeply interesting, but it's of course beyond the scope of this book.

Anyhow, there are also the greetings which have to do with the time of day. There is *buenos días (bwey-nohs di-ahs)*. This means literally "good morning" and is one of the more common Spanish greetings aside from *hola*. There also is *buenas tardes (bwey-nahs tar-dehs)*, which means *good evening*. This isn't used as often as a conventional salutation, though it certainly can be used as one with no problem. The last one in this category is *buenas noches (bwey-nahs no-chess)*. This means literally "good night" and its usage is unwavering; you will almost never ever use this as a salutation. You generally will only use this as a goodbye to somebody for the night is you know that you won't be seeing them again that night.

Lastly, there is *muy buenos. (moy bwey-nohs)*. This is a very general greeting as compared to other ones such as *buenos días* and *hola*. You can use this greeting at pretty much any time of day without anybody batting an eye.

So after all of that, we're now officially in the conversation, engaging in the nigh professional art of small talk. These small talk sessions generally almost always start by asking somebody how they are or how they're doing. There are a ton of ways to ask this sort of question in Spanish.

Firstly, there are the more formal and boring routes to be taken. To simply ask "How are you?", you first need to think about who you're talking to. Are you speaking to somebody your age? Younger? Older? Have you met them before? Then you need to pick either the informal or the formal way to ask based upon your evaluations. The informal way to ask is to simply "*¿Cómo estas?*" (co-moh es-tahs), meaning in a literal sense "how are you?". The formal way is just the usted inversion of the prior question: *¿Cómo está usted? (co-moh es-ta oos-ted)*. This means the same thing as before, but this version is of course to be reserved for meeting new people or for talking to people who are in a position of superiority.

On top of that, there are more casual ways to ask. You could say "how's it going?": *¿Cómo te va?* (co-moh teh va)

Simply asking "what's up?" is certainly not out of the question: *¿Qué tal?* (kay tall)

Neither would be asking something along the lines of "what's happening?"- *¿Qué pasa?* (kay pah-sah) - or "How have you been?": *¿Cómo has ido?* (co-moh ahs ee-do)

All in all, there are a ton of ways to ask somebody exactly how they're doing in Spanish. There are likewise a huge number of ways in which you could respond to this very question. Note that being in a foreign country or situation means that the culture is inevitably different; in America and England, when we ask "how are you?", we do so as a courtesy and generally not in the seeking of a very well-thought out response or any sort of genuine emotional discourse. Certain other countries aren't like this, and if you ask how they are, they'll tell you how they are.

But for all intents and purposes, you may or may not give a very deep response. Should you choose to go with a more "standard" response, there are a number of different ways in which you could phrase it.

You could start with the quintessential *bien, gracias* (byen, grah-see-as) which means simply "well/fine, thank you." You could also opt for "very well" by saying *muy bien* (moy byen). You could insert a certain amount of nihilistic apathy into your conversation by saying *Como siempre* which technically means "like always" but carries the weight more like "I am as I always seem to be." If you're not feeling well, you can say that you're sick by saying either *estoy enfermo* or *estoy enferma* depending upon your gender, men saying the first and women saying the second. And if you're not doing too well, you could say *más o menos* (moss oh men-ohs) meaning "so-so", or you could say *mal* which translates to simply "badly" or "poorly".

Then, there are multiple different ways in which you could say goodbye. There are a few generally used ones, and a few which are geared towards more special purposes.

The two general purpose ones that you need to know are *adiós* and *chao*. Both are common enough that I'm not going to tell you how to pronounce them. If you're on the up, you very well may notice a parallel between Spanish and neighboring Romance language Italian here, where *ciao* is used as a form of goodbye. Both of these are acceptable ways to say goodbye.

If you'll be seeing the person soon, you could tell them *Hasta pronto (ahs-tah pronto)*. But when I say *soon,* I mean **soon**. This is one place where the common conception of "soon" as used in the U.S. or Britain generally doesn't cut it in other timetables.

If you're just going to see them at a later point in time, you could say *Hasta luego (ahs-tah lwey-go)*. This could imply a lack of certainty about when you'll meet again, however. It, as many things do, ultimately depends upon the context in which it's used.

The last one we're going to talk about here is *Hasta la vista (ahs-tah lah vees-tah,* but honestly, who doesn't know how to pronounce this one thanks to Hollywood?). This phrase means essentially "Until next time" or "untill we meet again". This one too can communicate a lack of certainty dependent upon the context.

On top of all of that, there are some essential phrases that you have absolutely got to know in order to ask for help in Spanish, or otherwise get around.

Firstly, there are two forms of "excuse me" you need to know. The first, *perdón*, means "excuse me" in the sense of "excuse me, could I ask you about something?"

The other form of excuse me, *con permiso*, has a meaning more along the lines of "Please excuse me", when you're needing somebody to move out of your way.

You also need to know how to say thank you and sorry. In fact, more people need to know how to do this in their *native* language. The way that you say "thank you" in Spanish is straightforward: *Gracias*. Nearly everybody knows that term. And the way you say sorry is additionally simple: *Lo siento (lo syen-toh)*.

It's most certainly also worth you learning how to say *please* in Spanish because you invariably are going to need to at some point. You do so by saying *por favor. (pour fah-vor)*

And lastly, at some point, eventually you're going to have to ask for help in some way, shape, or form. The way to do this is by saying *necesito ayuda (ney-cess-ee-toh ah-you-dah)*. This means literally "I need help" or "I need aid". You'll also notice that this very simple phrase is built off of the verb *necesitar*, conjugated for the first person as worked with in chapter one.

There's a lot of things you'll need to learn before you're ready for the streets, but hopefully now, you've got a solid enough foundation you can at least be courteous.

Chapter 4: Pronouns Redux: Direct Object and Indirect Object

We spoke earlier in the book about the manifold uses of *subject pronouns* and how they're used in English in order to enrich our sentences and make them less monotonous or unwieldy, and how they're ditched almost entirely in Spanish after conjugating the verb due to their very verbose conjugation system.

It'd be a mortal sin for me to actually finish up this book and somehow leave out the idea of more advanced pronouns. You're going to inevitably end up needing to use these, and likely quite often. The manner by which we naturally speak English is absolutely littered with these things. They're peppered throughout essentially every sentence that we speak. The same manner of speaking applies to Spanish as well. Nobody on earth likes redundancy, and not having some kind of pronouns system in place not only endorses but *enforces* redundancy.

The first form of pronouns that we're going to focus on at this point in time are the *direct object pronouns*. Direct object pronouns are pronouns which stand in for the direct object of the sentence. In case you're unclear what a direct object is, it is the thing which takes the brunt of a verb or an action as indicated by the structure, context, and intention of the sentence.

I actually feel like before we jump into the *mechanics* of direct object pronouns, I should make the distinction between direct objects and indirect objects and why the distinction even really matters.

Direct objects are, as I said, objects which go along with the verb, whereas indirect objects are not. They are *affected* by the verb and the direct object, but they are in no way attached to them. The way that I like to say it is this: the sentiment of the sentence can completely and wholly exist even without the inclusion of the indirect object. It may be significantly vaguer, but the resultant thought is still a complete syntactically and grammatically correct sentence.

Take the following sentence for example:

I sent the card to her.

If we were to break this sentence down into its essential components, it would look as follows:

I - subject; indicates the person or thing which is actively undergoing the verb.

sent - verb; specifically a simple past verb which indicates that the person has already performed the given action.

the card - direct object; This is the thing

which is being directly affected by the verb. Without the verb *send*, there is no *the card* in this statement; without the *the card*, there is nothing to be *sent* in this statement. You can test the veracity of this by trying to rewrite the sentence without the direct object. "I am sending."/"I send." Great. What is being sent exactly? Without a direct object, these sentences make no sense.

to her. - indirect object; This is the thing which is being indirectly affected by the verb and is the end recipient of the consequences of the action of the verb. That is to say that the *indirect* object is non-essential where the *direct* object is essential. If you're ever confused in a sentence as to which is which, the first thing you should do is look for a preposition - indirect objects are usually sitting after a "to" or "at". However, the other thing you can do is try to rewrite the sentence once for each object without including the other. (In your head, if you'd like - doing it in real life would be rather wasteful.) The one which makes the least sense is invariably the one wherein the direct object has been removed. Compare "I sent the card." to "I sent to her." The only times that the second structure are permissible are when it's an idiomatic structure wherein the direct object is heavily implied or otherwise unneeded (consider the Victorian-era idiomatic phrasal verb "to send for [somebody]" meaning "to summon [somebody]", which has its roots in sending somebody like a messenger to go and get the person in question).

In other words, you will know which is the direct object and which isn't by which one can be taken out without the sentence losing any and all practical meaning.

So how do we express these sorts of pronouns in English? Well, let's shift our focus to the direct object pronouns again.

The way that we express direct object pronouns are by the use of pronouns such as "*me*", "*it*", "*him*", "*them*", and so forth. Let's take that sentence again. "I sent the card to her." *Her* is a indirect object pronoun because it replaces the traditional indirect object of the sentence which would be the *person's name*.

This indeed also turns this into a discussion of when you would use direct objects; the answer is after establishing relevancy for them. If a person or thing is mentioned by you or somebody else in a sentence, and that becomes the subject of the conversation, then you can by all means start to use object pronouns as heavily as you wish. If you fail to have some sort of initial object concept presented either by you or somebody else, all you're going to do is sound a tad bit confused at best or a tad bit crazy at worst.

Pro

In English, if I wanted to make this sentence simpler though, I could. Relatively easily too. Since we say "I sent the card" instead of "a card", we can boldly assume that the topic of conversation has already been established to be about both the card and the girl in question. So we could simplify this by replacing "the card" with the relevant direct object pronoun which would here be "it". So the sentence could become "I sent it to her." Following so far?

Spanish treats this sort of thing in a rather simple way. The Spanish layout for verbs and objects is flipped though. Their format for this sort of thing is as follows:

(subject) (indirect object) (direct object) (verb)

This format is often referred to as *SIODOV*.

There are several different direct object pronouns in Spanish. Their general meaning is as such:

Direct Object Pronouns

Pronoun	Meaning
Me	Me
Te	You
Lo	Him or It depending upon context
La	Her or It depending upon context
Nos	Us

Os	You (plural)
Los/las	Them

And the indirect object pronouns are very similar. Their only real difference is the dropping of gender in the third person pronouns.

Indirect Object Pronouns

Pronoun	Meaning
Me	Me
Te	You
Le/se	Him, Her, or It depending upon context
Nos	Us
Os	You (plural)
Les/se	Them

So let's go back to our example sentence, "I sent the card to her." When we write this in Spanish, before taking into account the direct object, we're going to transform "to her" into an indirect object, like so:

*I sent the card **to her**.*

*(Yo) **Le** envié la tarjeta.*

Yo is in parentheses because in virtually all forms of spoken and written Spanish, you'd drop the subject pronoun. If you didn't, then you'd risk sounding like you have no idea what you're saying and likewise have no business speaking Spanish in the first place.

Now, we can convert "la tarjeta" into a direct object pronoun so we're saying what is the Spanish equivalent of "I sent her it." or "I sent it to her." Super simple but pretty involving.

Since *la tarjeta* is a feminine noun, we need to use the third person singular feminine direct object pronoun. This would of course be *la*. And according to the presented rules of the *SIODOV* protocol, we're going to smush that in between our indirect object pronoun and our verb. So our sentence would come out like this:

(Yo) **le** la <u>envié</u>.

So we went from a massive and bulky sentence to something that's rather elegant. (Provided you have the appropriate context to make sense of a vague statement like "I sent her it" or "Le la envié.")

That draws this lesson on pronouns to an end, I'm afraid.

Conclusion

Thank for making it through to the end of *Learning Spanish: A Fast and Easy Guide for Beginners to Learn Conversational Spanish*, let's hope it was informative and able to provide you with all of the tools you need to achieve your goals whatever they may be.

The next step is to build upon the knowledge you've procured. As I'm sure you've noticed, my intent in this book wasn't to flood you over with vocabulary words or make you memorize a million things. Rather, my sole intent was that you walk away understanding the mechanical foundations of Spanish impeccably well.

The beauty of language is that it's the fundamental crux of civilization. There is no way that we could have developed anywhere near as far as we have had we not had the ability to communicate via spoken and written language. Truly, language is one of the most beautiful things in the universe.

That's why I feel so honored to have been afforded the opportunity to help you to understand Spanish better as you learn and go forward with it. My sincere hope is that I've given you at the very least a solid foundation that you can build *on top* of, because I know that my pet peeve with language learning books are those that fail to teach certain things in depth and are effectively trying to build a brick house on a very shaky foundation of linguistic knowledge.

And to be quite frank with you, I don't feel like that approach works, either. Only practice and immersion can make somebody a better language learner.

If at any point going forward with learning Spanish or French or Chinese or whatever that you may learn in the future, you feel that you're unable to full carry out your potential, or you feel that you just have hit a wall and can't go any further, then for me, quit lying to yourself. Absolutely anybody can learn another language. It takes time and work and dedication, often a lot more than most people have, but there are people born into bilingualism and trilingualism constantly. Not only that, but those same kids will often go on to learn yet *another* language later in life.

I guess the point that I'm trying to make here in closing is that my teaching method is a tad unorthodox because my whole belief in language learning is that giving you a long list of vocabulary words to memorize isn't the way to go about it; I genuinely feel that the only way for you to improve is through constant and concentrated effort being actively put forth towards a given language, and exerting energy in the general direction of making yourself better.

If you wish to flesh out your vocabulary, the way I earnestly recommend doing it is going to http://wordreference.com/enes/ and http://spanishdict.com/conjugate/ and working as hard as you can. Start writing a private blog or journal in order to learn new words and phraseologies. And, if you do find yourself wishing for more vocabulary-centric learning, I highly recommend Duolingo.

Finally, if you found this book useful in anyway, a review on Amazon is always appreciated!

Help me improve this book

While I have never met you, if you made it through this book I know that you are the kind of person that is wanting to get better and is willing to take on tough feedback to get to that point. You and I are cut from the same cloth in that respect. I am always looking to get better and I wish to not just improve myself, but also this book. If you have positive feedback, please take the time to leave a review. It will help other find this book and it can help change a life in the same way that it changed yours. If you have constructive feedback, please also leave a review. It will help me better understand what you, the reader, need to make significant improvements in your life. I will take your feedback and use it to improve this book so that it can become more powerful and beneficial to all those who encounter it.

REMEMBER TO JOIN THE GROUP NOW!

If you have not joined the Mastermind Self Development group yet, now is your time! You will receive videos and articles from top authorities in self development as well as a special group only offers on new books and training programs. There will also be a monthly member only draw that gives you a chance to win any book from your Kindle wish list!

If you sign up through this link http://www.mastermindselfdevelopment.com/specialreport you will also get a special free report on the Wheel of Life. This report will give you a visual look at your current life and then take you through a series of exercises that will help you plan what your perfect life looks like. The workbook does not end there; we then take you through a process to help you plan how to achieve that perfect life. The process is very powerful and has the potential to change your life forever. Join the group now and start to change your life! http://www.mastermindselfdevelopment.com/specialreport

91924344R00040

Made in the USA
Middletown, DE
03 October 2018